DRAGONS
YOUNG EXPLORER SERIES

IGUANIDS AND THEIR RELATIVES...

ERIK D. STOOPS

Faulkner's Publishing Group

This book is dedicated to Sherrie Stoops, a great mom. I love you.

Library of Congress Catalog Card Number 97-60523.

COVER PHOTO: Green Iguana by Terry Odegaard
DESIGNED BY: Graphic Arts & Production, Inc., Plover, WI

Faulkner's Publishing Group
200 Paw Paw Ave. #124
Benton Harbor, MI 49022

©1997 by Erik Daniel Stoops
Faulkner's ISBN 1-890475-01-7 Lib

Table of Contents

Chapter One

What are Iguanids and their Relatives?

What is an Iguanid?

How does a lizard shed its skin?

Read on to learn these answers and more.

What is an Iguanid?

An Iguanid is a reptile. These reptiles have four legs for climbing and swimming. They usually have a large powerful tail, eyelids and ears. Some lizards do not have legs at all. *Scientists* have found that certain lizard species are related to their cousin, the snake.

Are lizards cold-blooded or warm-blooded?

All species of lizards are *cold-blooded*. They need the warm sun during the day to help them move and digest their food.

THE GREEN IGUANA IS ONE OF ▶
THE MOST COMMON LIZARDS
FOUND IN THE WORLD.

by Terry Odegaard

5

Why does an Iguanid have scales?

Many kinds of lizards have different types of scales. Iguanids have smooth scales which are used to keep the lizards on their toes, while Horned Lizards have large rough scales which are used for protection against their enemies.

Why do lizards shed their skin?

All species of lizards shed their skin. When a lizard sheds its skin, that means it is growing. Some species of lizards such as Anoles shed in pieces, while other species like the Green Iguana may shed in one whole piece.

Why are their scales so many different colors?

Depending on where the lizard species lives, its scales may blend in with its surroundings. For example, the Green Iguana has green scales and is found in jungles and rain forests.

How does a lizard shed its skin?

When lizards shed their skin, they find something to rub on such as a rock or a tree branch. They try to wiggle out of their skin which usually takes a few hours. After a lizard sheds, it will have a bright new skin which is always shiny.

by Scottsdale Children's Nature Center

▲
THIS GREEN IGUANA IS SHEDDING ON HIS NOSE. WHEN A LIZARD SHEDS, IT IS A PART OF THE GROWING PROCESS.

What is the large scale on the bottom near the tail?

The large scale located between the back legs near the tail is called an ***anal plate***. This is where the lizards discharge their wastes, and also where their reproductive organs are located.

Can an Iguanid lose its tail?

Yes. Some species of lizards can lose their tail when they are frightened or get away from predators. The tail often grows back in a few months.

What is underneath all those scales?

Lizards have several layers of skin under all those scales.

THIS GREEN ▶ IGUANA'S SCALES PROTECT IT FROM MANY DIFFERENT CLIMATE CONDITIONS.

by Terry Odegaard

7

Horned Lizard:

The Horned Lizard or Horned Toad is found in southwestern United States. There is one species, the Short Horned Lizard, which can be found as far north as Canada. The tail is very short and the lizard is round and flat, outlined with small spines which are not sharp to the touch. Females can lay up to 20 eggs in midsummer and feed almost always on ants. They are famous for their blood-squirting eyes as a defense mechanism.

Marine Iguana:

One of the most interesting lizards in the world is the Marine Iguana. This is the only species of lizard that is actually a marine animal. Spending much of its time swimming in the ocean near the Galapagos Islands, the Marine Iguana feeds on algae and seaweed. Charles Darwin, on his voyage, spent a lot of time studying this lizard.

◀ THE MARINE IGUANA IS THE ONLY SPECIES OF LIZARD THAT HAS ADAPTED TO USE THE OCEAN TO SURVIVE.

by Clyde Peeling's Reptileland

8

by Terry Odegaard

THIS IS A PHOTO OF A SMALL GREEN IGUANA WHICH WILL GROW TO ADULT SIZE IN A FEW YEARS.

Green Iguana:

This is a common lizard from parts of Central and South America. They are very popular pets in the United States. They can grow up to 6 1/2 feet in length and feed on a variety of items including vegetables and plant material as well as animals they catch. They use their powerful tail as a defense strategy. A female can lay up to 30 eggs at one time.

Rhinoceros Iguana:

One of the strangest Iguanid species is the Rhinoceros Iguana. They have three horny protuberances (horned plates) on the tip of their snout. They live in Haiti in open, dry country. They feed on plants and animals found in the area. This lizard is an *endangered* species. According to scientists, this lizard may become extinct by the turn of the century if special breeding programs and laws are not enacted to protect these animals in the wild state.

THIS IS A PHOTO OF A FEMALE RHINOCEROS ◀ IGUANA.

by Terry Odegaard

Chuckwalla:

The Chuckwalla is one of the most impressive species of lizards. They are found in southwestern United States and parts of Mexico. They like to spend their time between large slabs of rocks and boulders where they feel safe. When frightened, they blow up their loose flaps of skin with air and wedge themselves between the rocks. It looks like a balloon with feet and a head. They feed on small desert flowers and plants. Their skin feels like sandpaper.

by Terry Odegaard ▲ CHUCKWALLA

THE GREEN BASILISK ▶ IS ONE OF THE MOST BEAUTIFUL LIZARDS IN THE WORLD.

by
Pat
Turcott

Basilisk:

One of the most awesome looking lizards is the Double Crested Basilisk. They are green all over with small blue dots and yellow eyes, plus they look like they have fins on their head. They are one of the only species of lizards that can run so fast they have been known to run across water. They feed on small animals and fruit. They can grow up to 3 feet in size.

10

Sungazer:

Sungazers are not Iguanids but are related to them. They are in their own family. The Sungazer is found in southern Africa. They have large spines along their back which may be used as weapons. They are called Sungazers because they love basking in the sun on large rocks and termite mounds. They feed on insects.

SUNGAZER ▶

by Terry Odegaard

by Terry Odegaard

▲ SUNGAZER

11

Chapter Two

Where are Iguanids and their Relatives Found?

Where do Iguanids live?

Can Iguanids swim?

Read on to find these answers and more.

Where do Iguanids live?

Lizards are distributed all over the world. The greatest number of species are found in the warm zones: deserts, jungles, rain forests, etc. The only place you cannot find a lizard is in the ice-covered polar regions and where temperatures remain ice-cold year-round.

THE THICK RAIN FOREST OF COSTA RICA IS HOME TO MANY SPECIES OF IGUANIDS. THE SONORAN DESERT IS HOME TO THE DESERT IGUANA AND THE CHUCKWALLA.

by Terry Odegaard

MANY SPECIES OF LIZARDS MAKE THEIR HOMES IN LARGE TREES LIKE THIS ONE.

Where is the best place to find an Iguanid?

If I were a lizard, this is where I would be:

- Under a rock
- On a rock
- In a field
- On a house
- In a tree
- In a rain forest

Can Iguanids swim?

Some species of lizards are great swimmers such as the Water Dragon. They use their legs and tail to help them glide in the water.

Can lizards climb trees?

Yes. Tree Lizards of southwestern United States deserts spend much of their lives in trees and are found to be wonderful climbers.

13

Chapter Three

Senses and Self-Defense

Lizards bite if they are afraid.

Some lizards play dead if they are afraid and some hiss, while others have great hoods on their neck.

This chapter will answer some of the important questions about lizards' senses and self-defense.

Do Iguanids sleep?

Yes. Some species of lizards sleep at night such as the Green Iguana, while others such as some species of Anoles sleep during the day and are active all night long.

by Terry Odegaard

▲ THIS PHOTOGRAPH OF A FENCE LIZARD WAS TAKEN AT NIGHT. THIS LIZARD IS SLEEPING.

Do Iguanids have eyelids?

Yes. Unlike snakes, all species of lizards have eyelids. Like our eyelids, they protect the lizard's eyes from dirt and predators.

Can lizards see colors?

Scientists have found that certain species of lizards can see colors, such as red and yellow. Many scientists are still learning about these spectacular findings.

◀ IF YOU LOOK CLOSELY AT THIS RHINOCEROS IGUANA YOU WILL SEE THAT THEY HAVE EYELIDS LIKE WE DO.

by Terry Odegaard

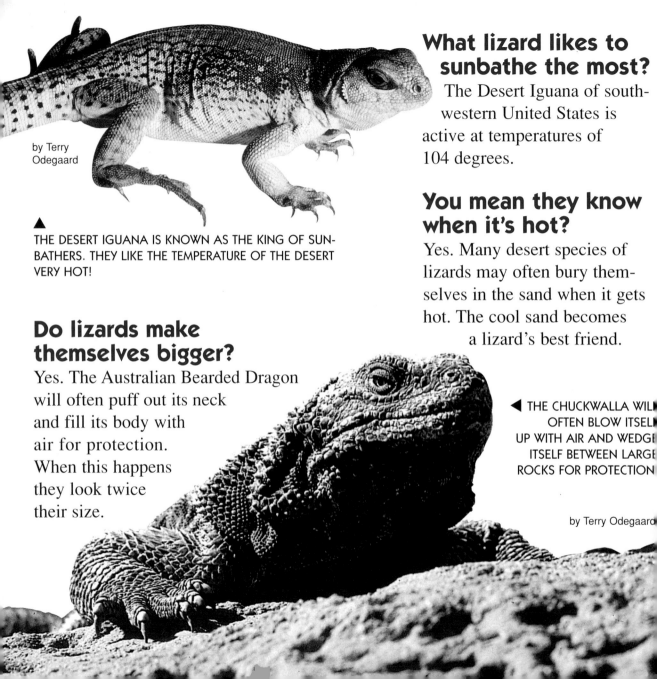

by Terry Odegaard

▲
THE DESERT IGUANA IS KNOWN AS THE KING OF SUN-BATHERS. THEY LIKE THE TEMPERATURE OF THE DESERT VERY HOT!

What lizard likes to sunbathe the most?

The Desert Iguana of south-western United States is active at temperatures of 104 degrees.

You mean they know when it's hot?

Yes. Many desert species of lizards may often bury them-selves in the sand when it gets hot. The cool sand becomes a lizard's best friend.

Do lizards make themselves bigger?

Yes. The Australian Bearded Dragon will often puff out its neck and fill its body with air for protection. When this happens they look twice their size.

◄ THE CHUCKWALLA WILL OFTEN BLOW ITSELF UP WITH AIR AND WEDGE ITSELF BETWEEN LARGE ROCKS FOR PROTECTION

by Terry Odegaard

Why do lizards bite?

If you picked up a lizard in the wild it might bite. That is why we should never pick up a lizard in the wild. Lizards often bite if they are frightened. Some will bite to defend themselves against other lizards and enemies.

by Terry Odegaard

Do lizards do push-ups?

Yes. Male lizards are territorial and will often bob their head up and down. Thus, they do push-ups on a rock to show authority. It looks very funny when they do this.

How do they play dead?

The Greater Earless Lizard of south-western United States may often play dead when captured. They will lie motionless until they feel unthreatened.

How do lizards protect themselves?

Some species, such as the Frilled Dragon will often spread the hood on its neck to scare off their enemies. Others hiss and open their mouth like the Gila Monster.

◄ THIS MALE SUNGAZER IS DOING PUSH-UPS. THEY WILL DO THIS TO PROTECT THEIR TERRITORY FROM OTHER LIZARDS. THE SUNGAZER ALSO USES ITS LARGE SPINES AND SCALES TO PROTECT ITSELF FROM ITS ENEMIES.

by Terry Odegaard

Chapter Four

Eating Habits

What do Iguanids eat?

Do lizards get fat?

Read on to learn these answers and more.

What do Iguanids eat?

Lizards eat many different things like mammals, reptiles, insects, fish and snails. Each species has its own type of food it eats. For example, Tree Lizards like to eat flies, while Green Iguanas eat fruits and vegetables.

Do lizards get fat?

In captivity, Iguanid species that do not get very much exercise often become overweight. This is not healthy for lizards and can cause diseases.

How do lizards capture their food?

Lizards use their eyesight and their strong sense of smell to find their food. Insect-eating lizards may stay at a cricket nest and feed until all are full.

by Terry Odegaard ▲
THIS RHINOCEROS IGUANA IS ENJOYING A BANANA LUNCH.

GREEN IGUANA ▶

by Terry Odegaard

19

Chapter Five

Lizard Reproduction

Some species of lizards lay eggs,
while other species give live birth.

Do lizards make good parents?

Do lizards stay as a couple?

Read on and try to find the answers.

How do you tell the difference between the male and female?

In some species of lizards, males may be more colorful or larger than the females.
In other species such as Geckos, males may have larger tails than females.
Male lizards have hemi-penes located in the anal plate and used for mating.

When do Iguanids mate?

Iguanids mate depending on the species and where
it is found during the spring or rainy season.

THIS YOUNG GREEN IGUANA IS A
FEMALE. WE CAN TELL THIS BY THE
SMALL SPINES ALONG HER BACK.
▼

by Terry Odegaard

22

Will male lizards fight for the female?

Yes. Males will often court potential females and may often show signs of display to impress the female. In Iguanid species, males may often fight one another for the right to mate. The fight might look bad, but it is rarely fatal.

Do Iguanids give live birth?

They give birth the same way as egg-laying species, through the anal plate. The *neonates*, "newborns," will often be born in an egg yolk placenta sack, which they usually break out of when born. Baby lizards use their egg tooth to do this. The egg tooth usually falls off in about a week. Sometimes the mother lizard will eat the placenta sacks. This provides nutrition for the exhausted mother lizard.

by Terry Odegaard

Do lizards lay eggs?

As an egg-laying species, the Bearded Dragon often will bury her eggs in a safe, warm, moist place. Lizards lay eggs through their anal plate. Some lizards can lay up to 30 eggs.

Do Iguanids make good parents?

No. Most species do not. After their young are born, the mother may never see the offspring again.

23

Chapter Five

Facts about Iguanids and their Relatives

What does endangered mean?

Do lizards squirt blood?

This chapter covers the most interesting questions
we all have about the lizard.

WHEN PICKED UP, THE HORNED LIZARD HAS A STRANGE DEFENSE. THEY CAN FRIGHTEN OFF THEIR ENEMIES BY SQUIRTING BLOOD FROM THEIR EYES.

AFTER THIS HORNED TOAD SQUIRTED BLOOD FROM ITS EYES, WE PLACED IT BACK ON THE GROUND AND IT RAN AWAY SAFELY.

THE HORNED LIZARD IS THE ONLY LIZARD THAT CAN SQUIRT BLOOD FROM ITS EYES.

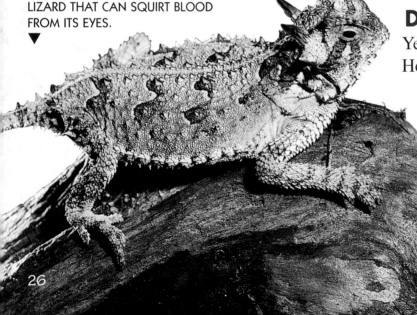

Do lizards squirt blood?

Yes. The Horned Lizard or Horned Toad has a remarkable way of scaring its enemies. This is one of the strangest things in all of the animal world. From the corner of each eye, they can shoot a thin stream of blood when frightened. This does not hurt the lizard and it will not hurt you.

by Terry Odegaard

Can lizards change colors?

Yes. There are several lizard species that can change color. One is called the Carolina Anole. This little lizard is often kept as a pet.

by Terry Odegaard

What does endangered species mean?

The word **endangered** means a species threatened with extinction. Every day a number of species of animals becomes endangered or even becomes extinct.

THE GALAPAGOS ISLANDS IGUANA ▶
IS AN ENDANGERED SPECIES.
THERE ARE MANY GOVERN-
MENTS WORLDWIDE THAT
ARE PROTECTING
THIS RARE
LIZARD.

by Terry Odegaard

If we see a lizard in the wild, what should we do?

The best thing to do is to leave it alone. Many kinds of lizards like to eat the bugs around your house. This is a very good thing and you should enjoy the wonderful opportunity to view these great creatures.

Do lizards puff smoke?

Yes. Marine Iguanas have been known to puff a kind of steam from their nose when frightened. What this really is, is salt build up from the nose. They spend so much time in the sea that the salt builds up and they puff it out.

by Terry Odegaard

◀ THE DESERT ROCK AREA IS HOME TO CHUCKWALLAS AND DESERT IGUANAS. IF YOU SEE A LIZARD IN YOUR AREA, THE BEST THING TO DO IS LET IT BE.

29

Glossary

Anal Plate:
The large scale between the back legs of the lizard.

Chlamydosaurus King II:
A scientific name for frilled lizard.

Cold-Blooded:
Having a body temperature not internally regulated, but approximately that of the environment.

Endangered: Threatened with extinction.

Endemic:
Native to a particular country, nation or region.

External:
Having merely the outward appearance of something.

Fossil:
A remnant impression, or trace of an animal or plant of past geological ages that has been preserved in the earth's crust.

Herpetologist:
One who studies reptiles and amphibians.

Neonate: Newborn.

Paleontologist:
One who studies the science dealing with the life of past geological periods as known from fossil remains.

Parasite:
An organism that lives in or on another organism at whose expense it receives nourishment.

Poacher:
One who kills or takes game and fish illegally.

Quadrupole:
A system composed of two dipoles of equal but oppositely directed moment.

Rhynchocephalian:
A class of reptile.

Scientist:
A scientific investigator.

Unisexual:
All individuals are females that can lay eggs and are fertile without mating.

Virus:
The causative agent of an infectious disease.

Warm-Blooded:
Having a relatively high and constant body temperature relatively independent of the surroundings.

Books and CD-Roms Written by the Author Suggested Reading

Snakes and Other Reptiles of the Southwest

Erik D. Stoops & Annette T. Wright. 1991. Golden West Publishing Company, Phoenix, Arizona. Scientific Field Guide.

Snakes

Erik D. Stoops & Annette T. Wright. 1992. Hardback and Paperback. Sterling Publishing Company, New York. Children's non-fiction, full-color, question and answer format. First Book in Children's Nature Library Series.

Breeding Boas and Pythons

Erik D. Stoops & Annette T. Wright. 1993. TFH Publishing Company, New York. Scientific Care and Breeding Guide.

Sharks

Erik D. Stoops & Sherrie L. Stoops. Illustrated by Jeffrey L. Martin. June, 1994. Hardback and Paperback. Sterling Publishing Company, New York. Children's non-fiction, full-color, question and answer format. Second Book in Children's Nature Library Series.

Dolphins

Erik D. Stoops, Jeffrey L. Martin & Debbie L. Stone. Release date, January, 1995. Hardback and Paperback. Sterling Publishing Company, New York. Children's non-fiction, full-color, question and answer format. Third Book in Children's Nature Library Series.

Whales

Erik D. Stoops, Jeffrey L. Martin & Debbie L. Stone. Release date, March, 1995. Hardback and Paperback. Sterling Publishing Company, New York. Children's non-fiction, full-color, question and answer format. Fourth Book in Children's Nature Library Series.

Scorpions and Other Venomous Insects of the Desert

Erik D. Stoops & Jeffrey L. Martin. Release date, June, 1995. Golden West Publishing Company, Phoenix, Arizona. A user-friendly guide.

Alligators and Crocodiles

Erik D. Stoops & Debbie L. Stone. Release date, October, 1994. Sterling Publishing Company, New York. Children's non-fiction, full-color, question and answer format. Fifth Book in Children's Nature Library Series.

Wolves

Erik D. Stoops & Dagmar Fertl. Release date, December, 1996. Sterling Publishing Company, New York. Children's non-fiction, full-color, question and answer format. Sixth Book in Children's Nature Library Series.

Internet Sites:

Zoo Net:
http://www.mindspring.com/~zoonet

Herp Link:
http://home.ptd.net/~herplink/index.html

Erik Stoops:
http://www.primenet.com/~dink

Look for the Adventures of Dink the Skink Children's book series and animated CD Rom Stories coming out in 1997.

INDEX

WE WOULD LIKE TO THANK THE FOLLOWING PEOPLE FOR THEIR ENCOURAGEMENT AND PARTICIPATION:
NATIONAL ZOOLOGICAL PARK, OFFICE OF PUBLIC AFFAIRS, SUSAN BIGGS, SMITHSONIAN INSTITUTION, TERRY CHRISTOPHER, TERRY ODEGAARD, CINCINNATI ZOO AND BOTANICAL GARDENS, ST. LOUIS ZOO, BILL LUBACK'S REPTILES, INC., AMANDA JAKSHA, JESSIE COHEN, PAT TURCOTT, RODNEY FREEMAN, DIANE E. FREEMAN, STEVEN CASTANEDA, CLYDE PEELINGS OF REPTILELAND, MICKEY OLSEN OF WILDLIFE WORLD ZOO, SCOTTSDALE CHILDREN'S NATURE CENTER, DR. JEAN ARNOLD, ARIZONA GAME AND FISH DEPARTMENT, ERIN DEAN OF THE UNITED STATES FISH AND WILDLIFE SERVICE, BOB FAULKNER, DAVE PFEIFFER OF EDUCATION ON WHEELS FOR MAKING THIS PROJECT A REALITY, DR. MARTY FELDMAN, SHERRIE STOOPS, ALESHA STOOPS, VICTORIA AND JESSICA EMERY.